PAISLEYS
AND OTHER
TEXTILE DESIGNS
FROM INDIA

K. Prakash

DOVER PUBLICATIONS, INC.
New York

Bibliographical Note

This Dover edition, first published in 1994, is an unabridged republication of the second edition of *Impressions: A Classic Collection of Textile Designs,* published in 1992 by K. Prakash, Bombay, India.

DOVER *Pictorial Archive* SERIES

This book belongs to the Dover Pictorial Archive Series. You may use the designs and illustrations for graphics and crafts applications, free and without special permission, provided that you include no more than ten in the same publication or project. (For permission for additional use, please write to Dover Publications, Inc., 180 Varick Street, New York, N.Y. 10014.)
However, republication or reproduction of any illustration by any other graphic service whether it be in a book or in any other design resource is strictly prohibited.

Library of Congress Cataloging-in-Publication Data

Prakash, K.
    [Impressions]
    Paisleys and other textile designs from India / K. Prakash.
        p.   cm.—(Dover pictorial archive series)
    "An unabridged republication of the second edition of Impressions: a classic collection of textile designs, published in 1992 by K. Prakash, Bombay, India"—T.p. verso.
    ISBN 0-486-27959-6 (pbk.)
    1. Paisley design—India—Themes, motives. 2. Textile design—India—Themes, motives. I. Title. II. Series.
NK1575.P73 1994
745.4′4954—dc20   93–39105
                                                                                    CIP

Manufactured in the United States of America
Dover Publications, Inc., 31 East 2nd Street, Mineola, N.Y. 11501

Publisher's Note

From ancient traditions of Indian art and handicraft, K. Prakash has created this unique collection of textile designs. *Paisleys and Other Textile Designs from India* contains 144 pages of ornamental design patterns collected from India's different regions, such as Banaras, center of fine arts and exquisitely designed fabrics, as well as Kashmir, Punjab and other parts of North and South India. In addition to the rich floral patterns, this collection features unique paisleys, a pattern with roots in Mughal art and one that is as popular today as when it was introduced to the West in the early eighteenth century.

Each design is clearly printed, featuring a wealth of intricate details that will make this book an invaluable resource for fashion designers, fabric painters, embroiderers and other textile artists.

PAISLEYS
AND OTHER
TEXTILE DESIGNS
FROM INDIA

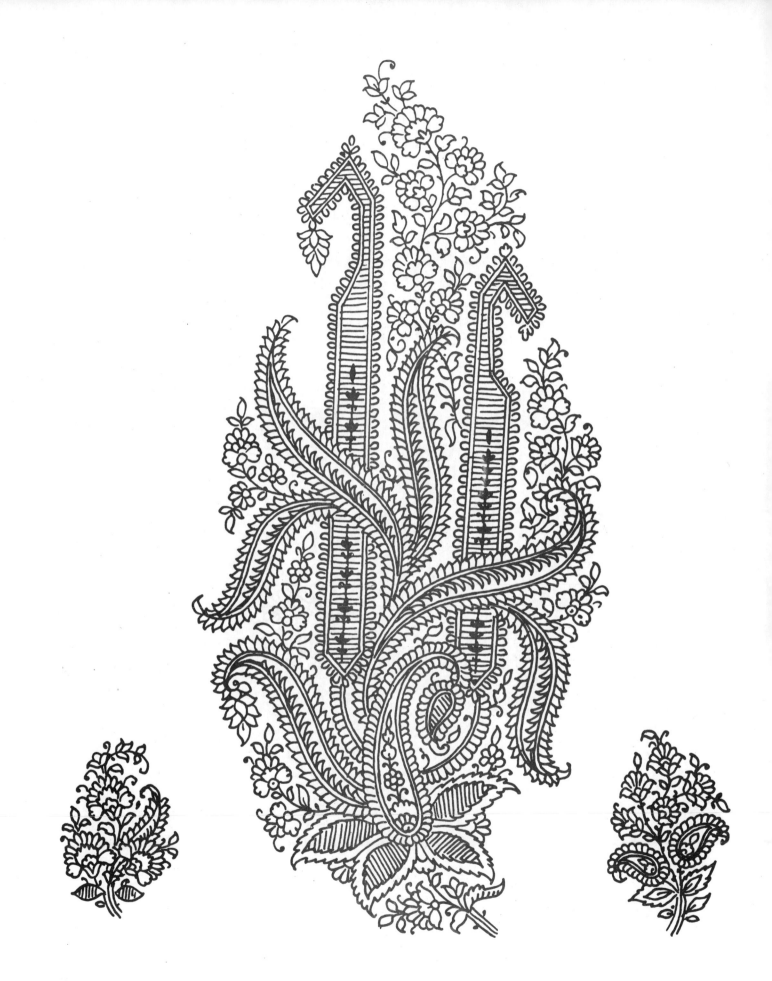

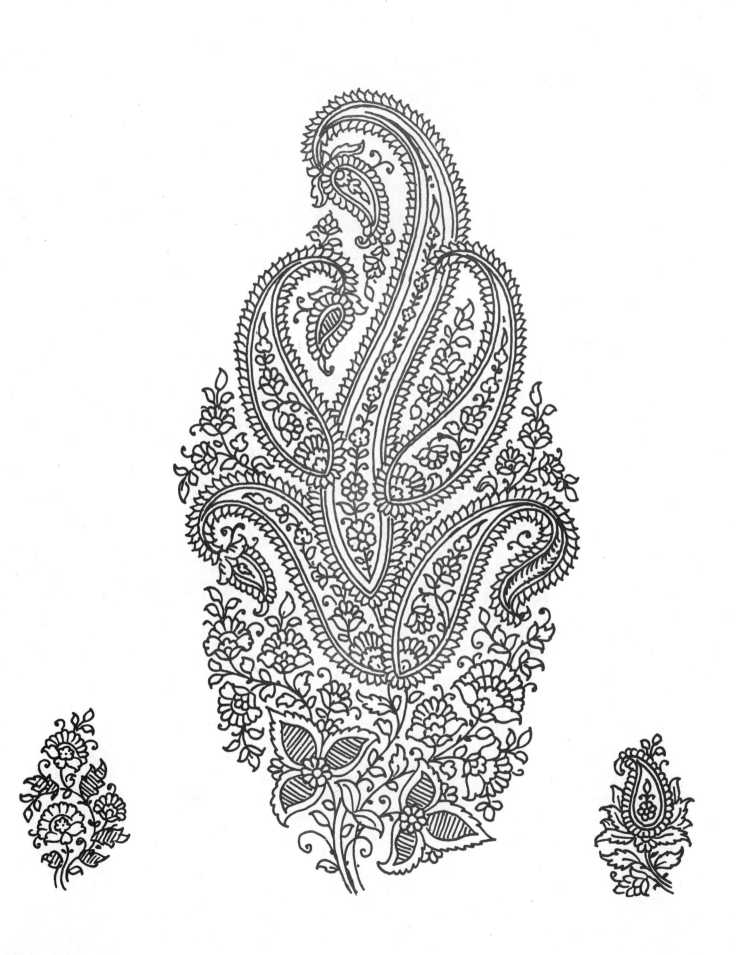

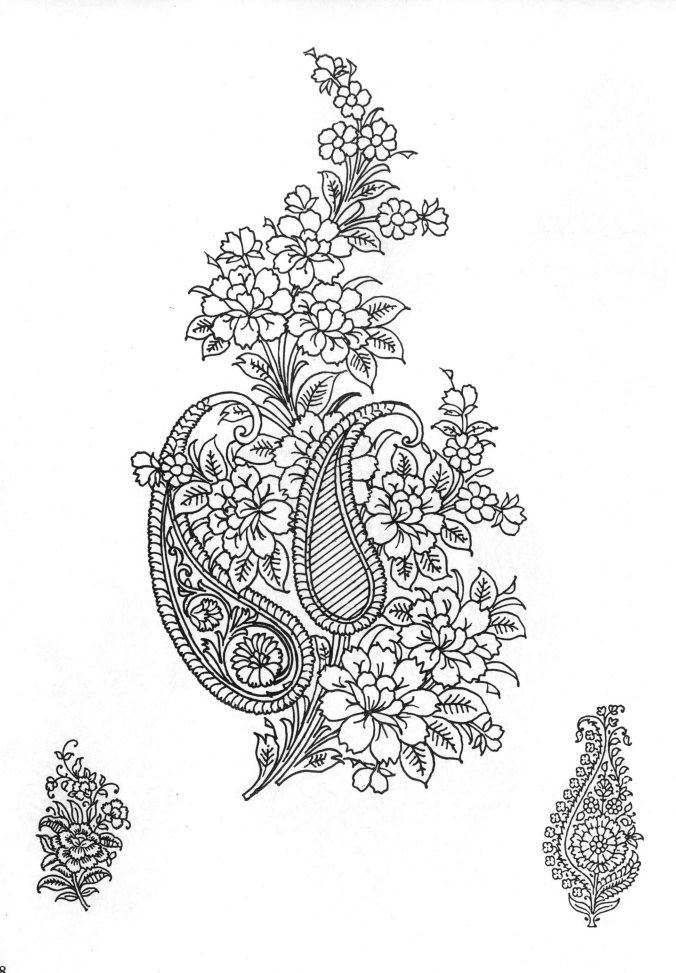

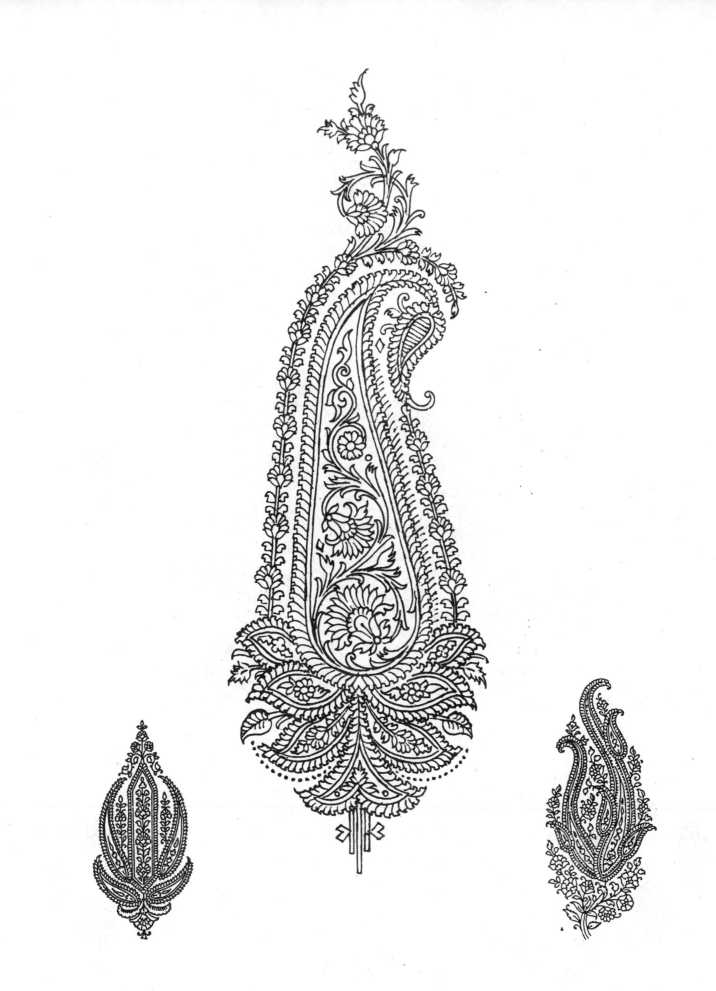

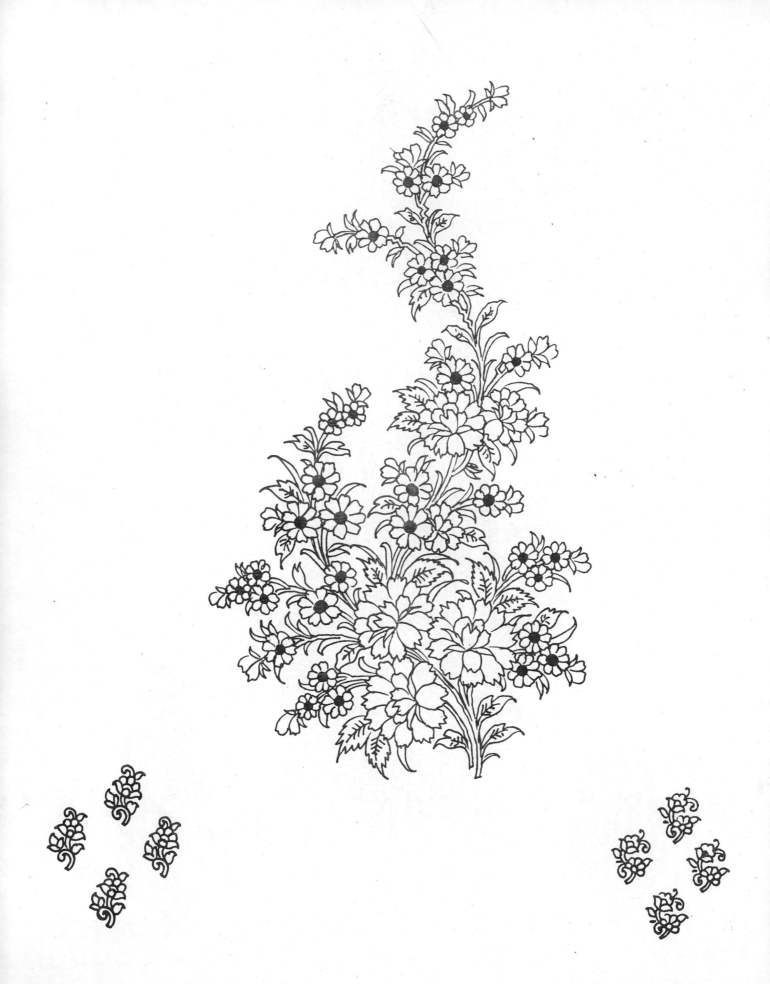

30

34

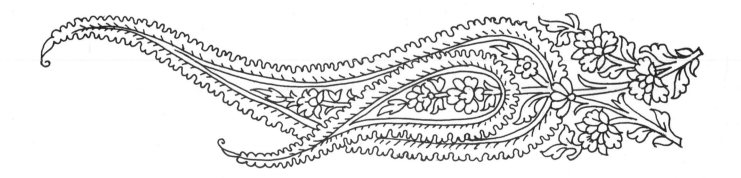

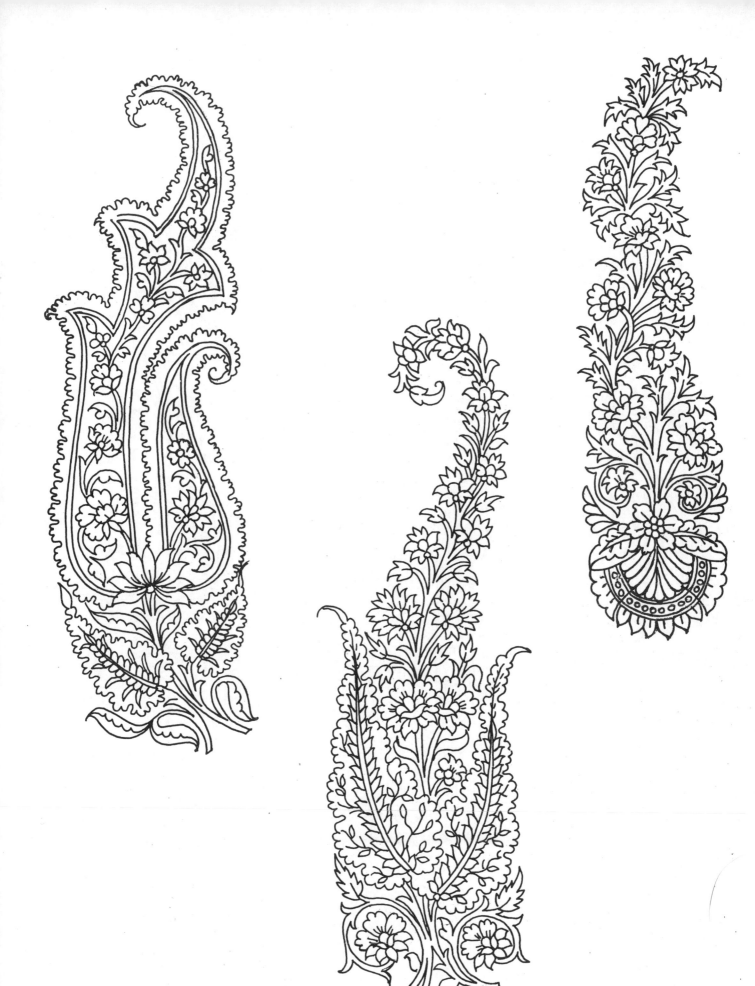

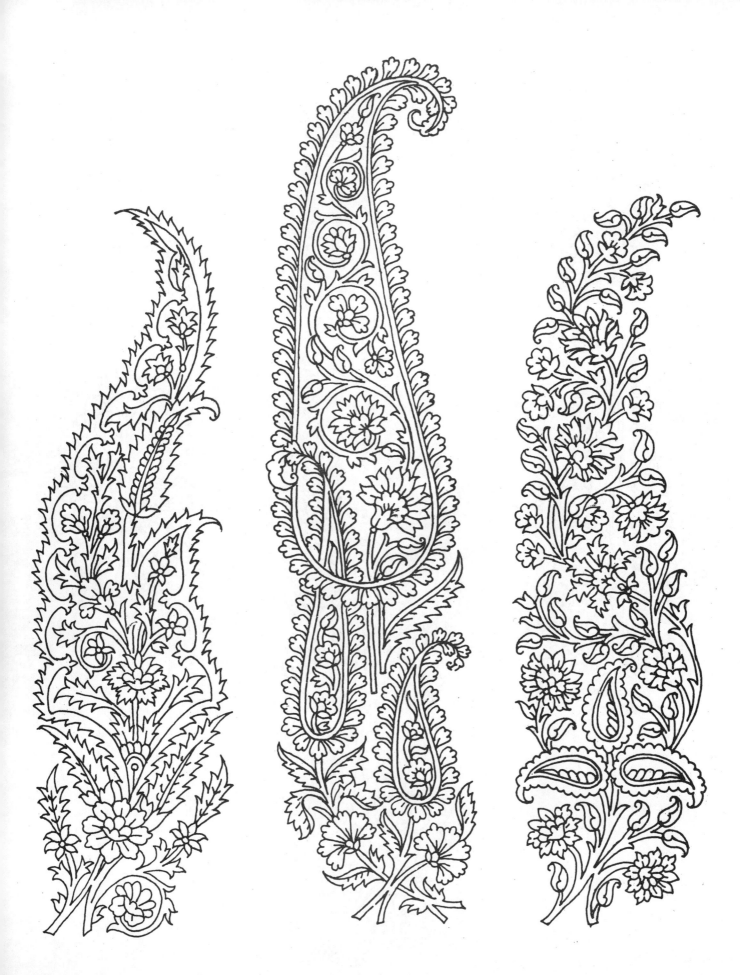

44

58

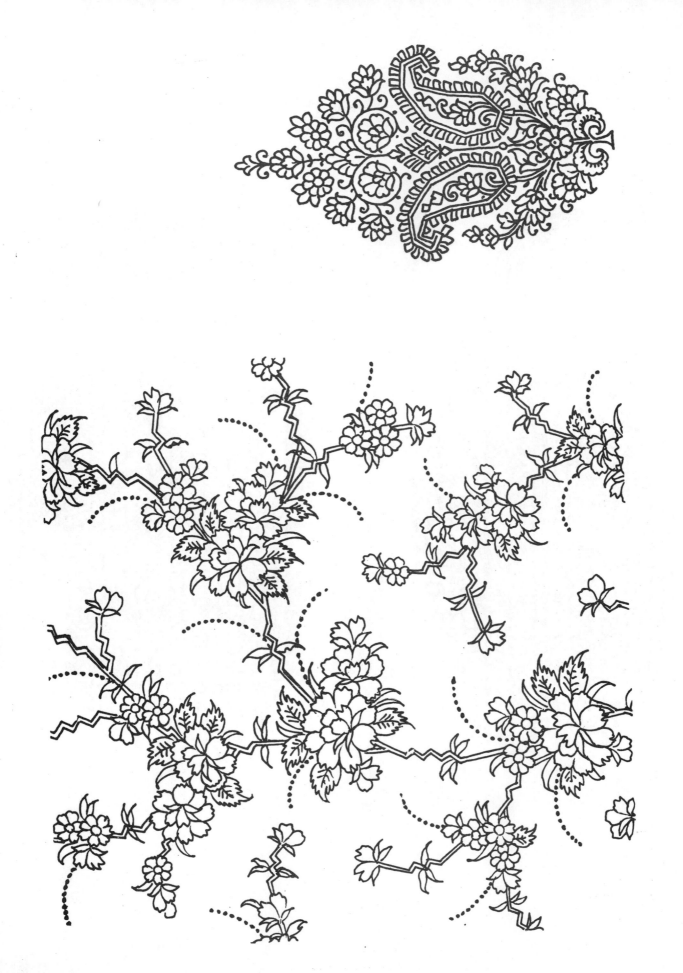

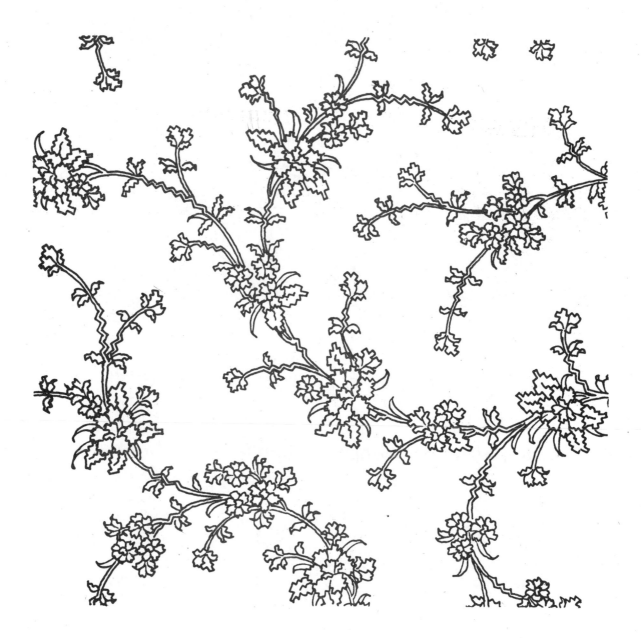

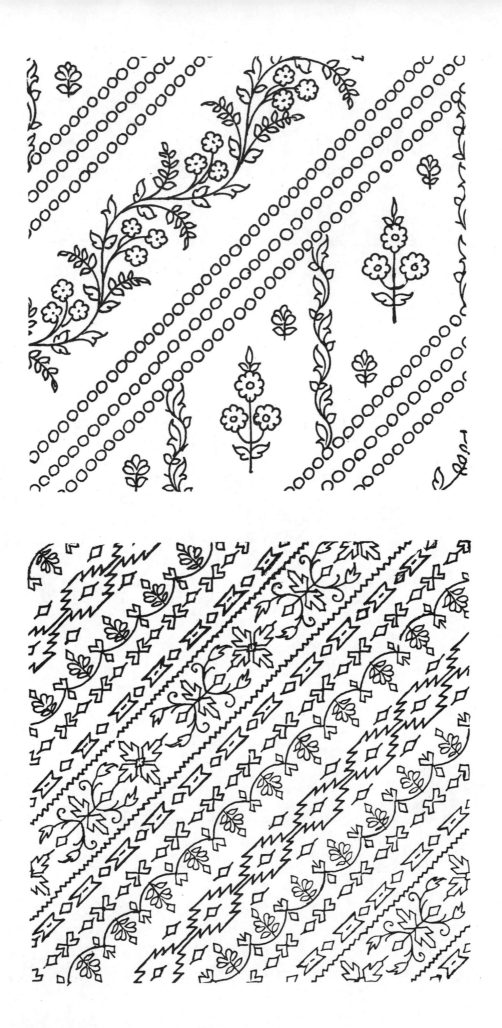

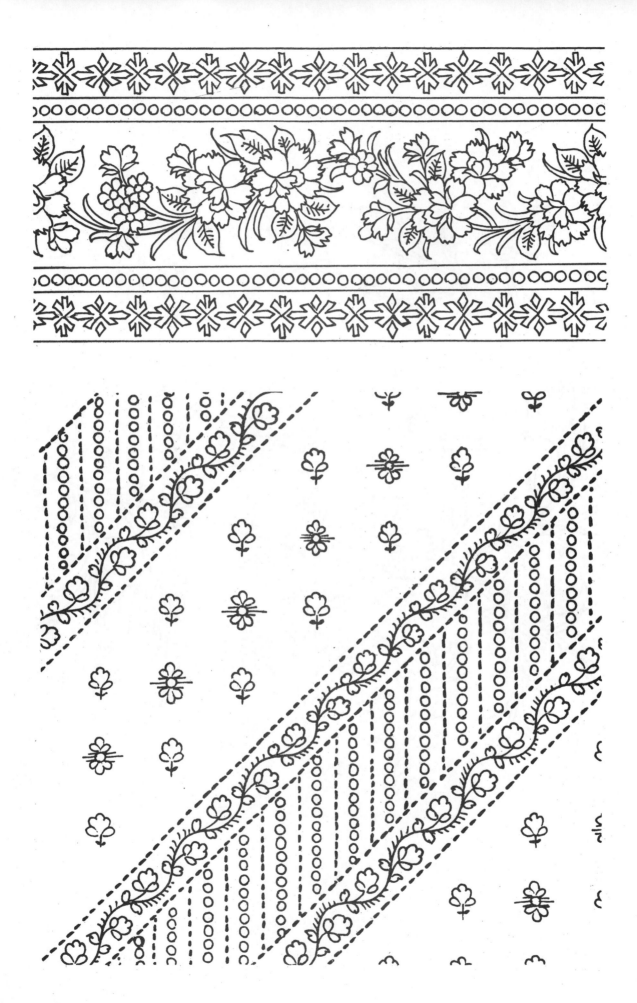

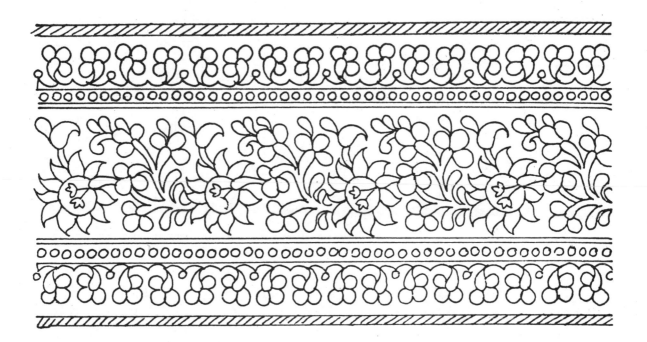

87

90

91

92

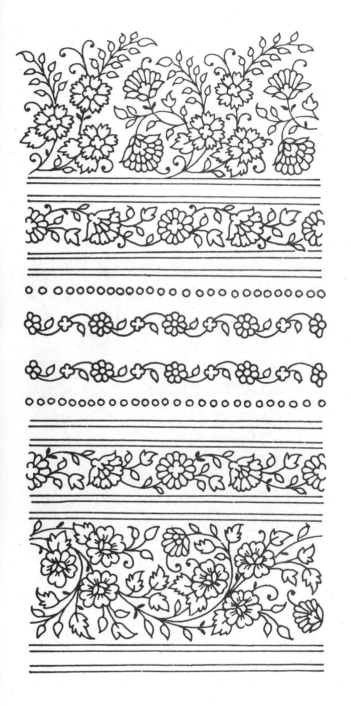

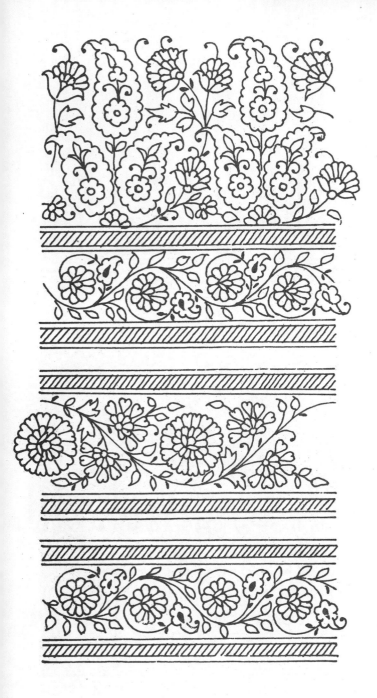

99

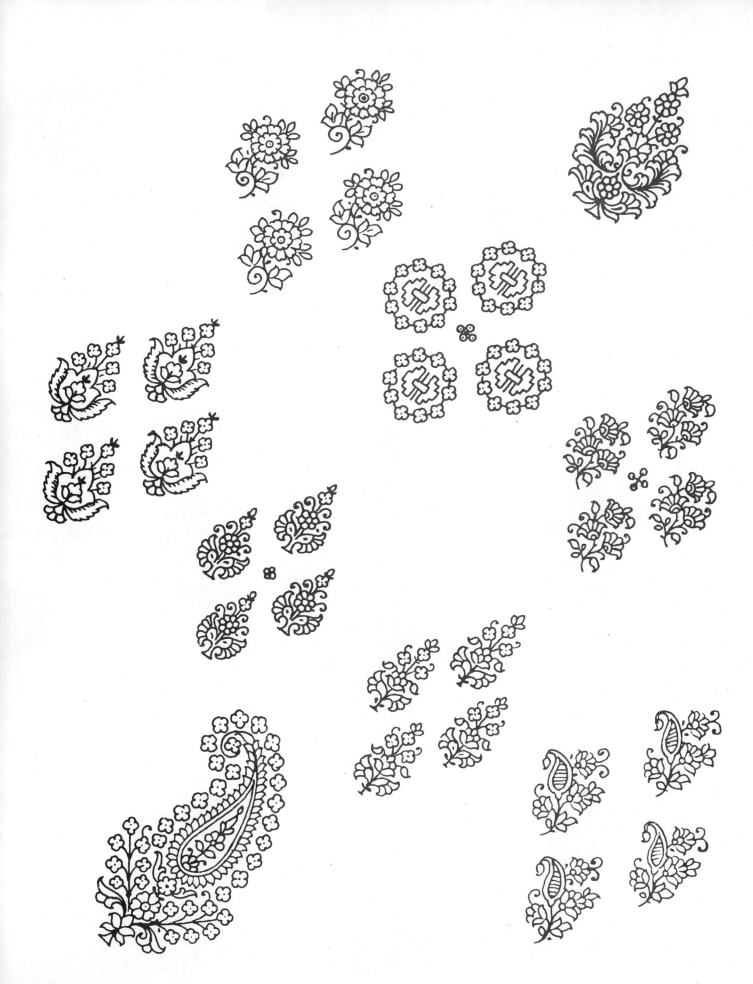

113

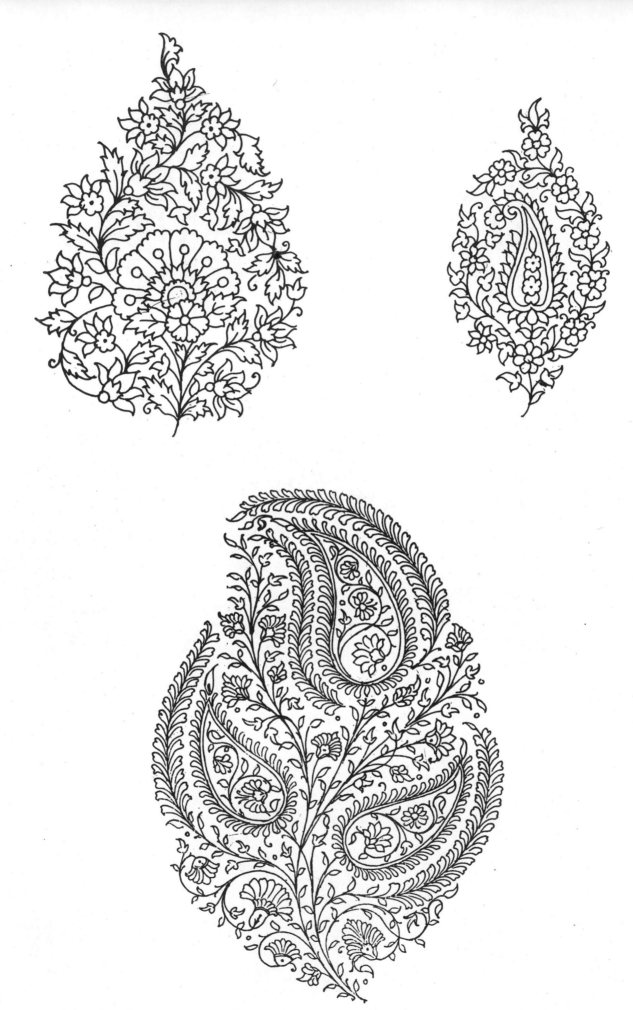

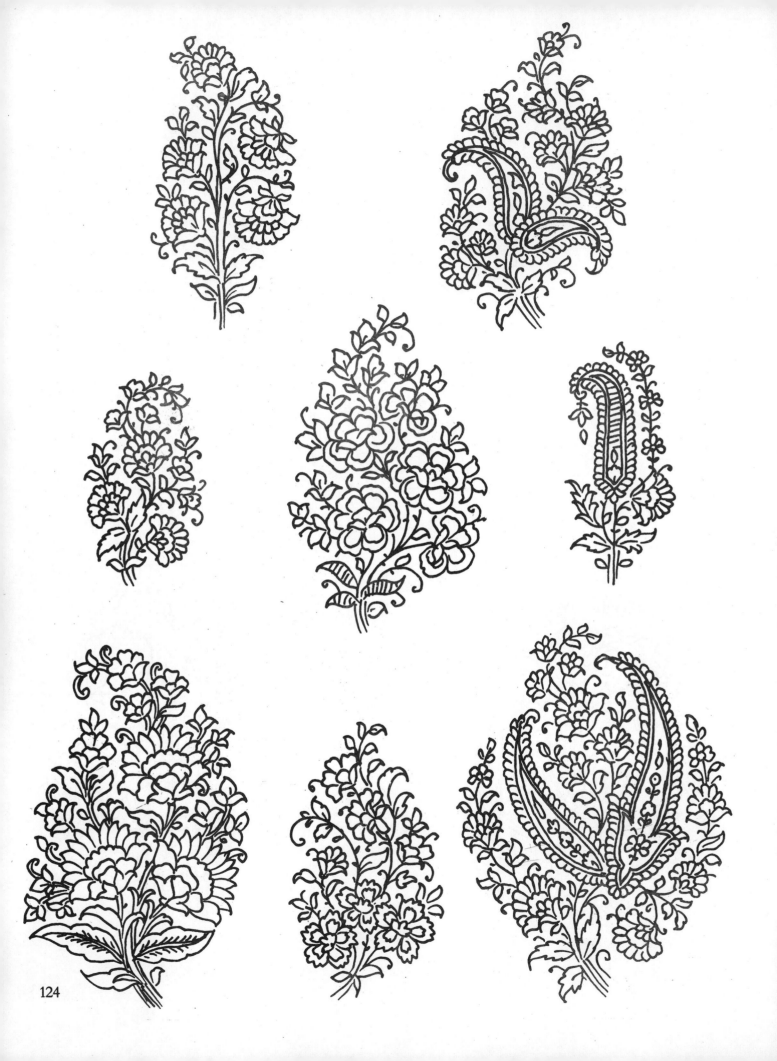

124

125

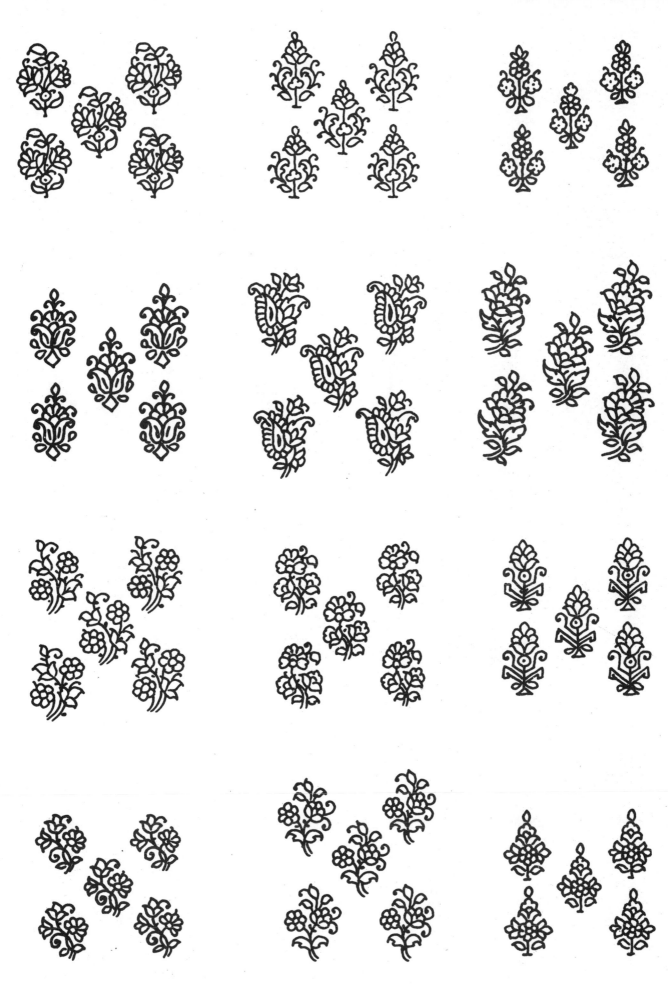

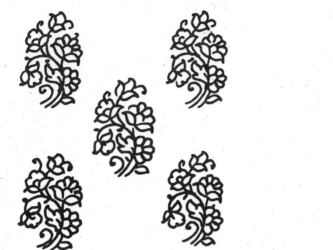

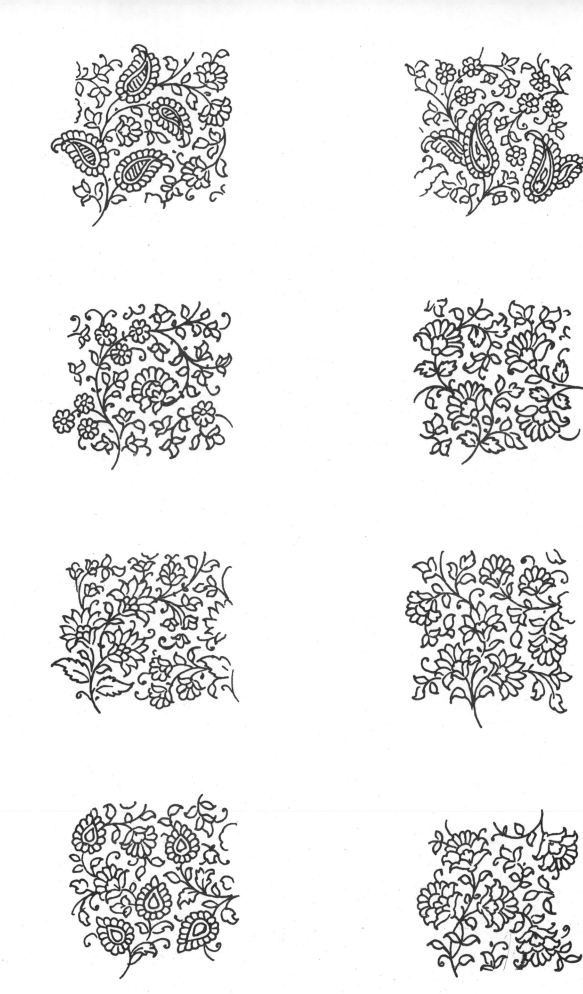

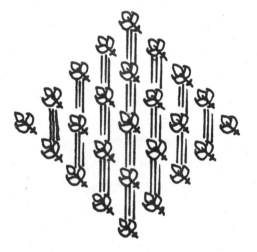 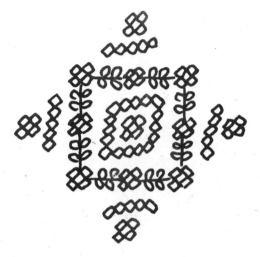

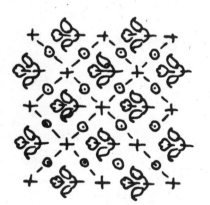

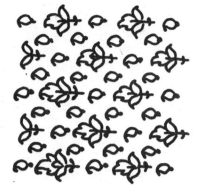

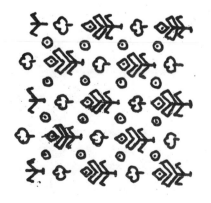

138

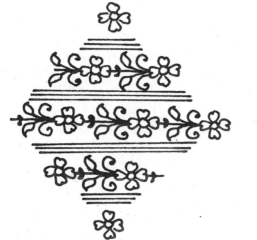

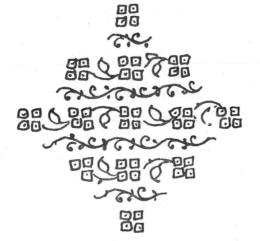

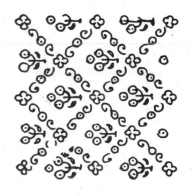

139

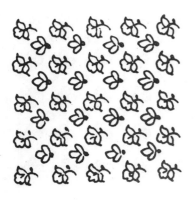

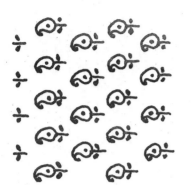

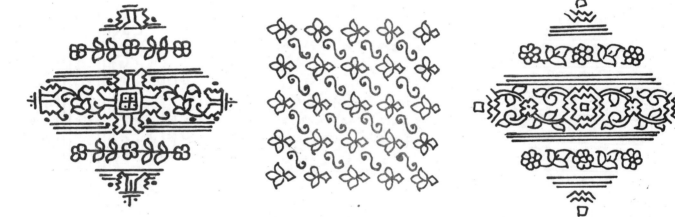

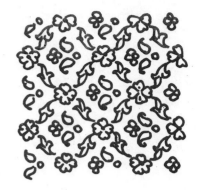

142

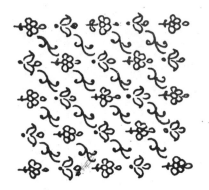

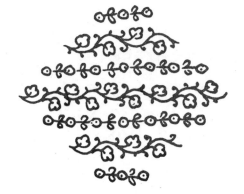

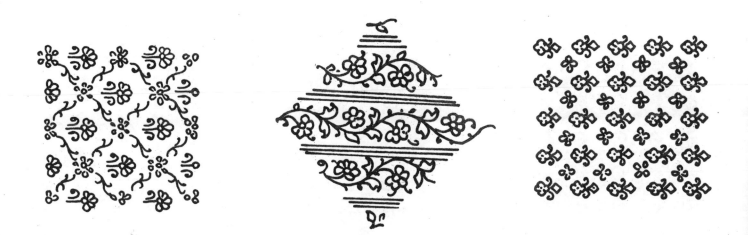

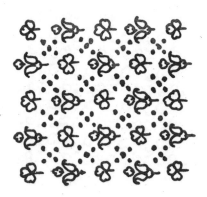

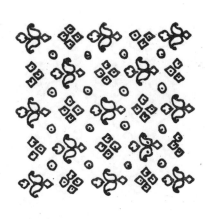